V-2
ROCKETS

by
Paula Younkin

Crestwood House
New York

Maxwell Macmillan Canada
Toronto

Maxwell Macmillan International
New York   Oxford   Singapore   Sydney

Library of Congress Cataloging-in-Publication Data
Younkin, Paula

V-2 Rockets / Paula Younkin. — 1st ed.
j.   cm. — (Those daring machines)
Includes bibliographical references and index.
Summary: The story of the V-weapons, Nazi Germany's terrifying rockets of war.
ISBN 0-89686-827-3   **0-382-24765-5 (pbk.)**
1. V-2 rocket — Juvenile literature.   2. World War, 1939-1945 — Aerial operations, German — Juvenile literature.   3. Rockets (Aeronautics) — Juvenile literature.   4. Brain drain — Germany — History — 20th century — Juvenile literature. I. Title. II. Series.
D787.Y59 1994
940.54'4943 — dc20   94-18475

Crestwood House
Macmillan Publishing Company
866 Third Avenue
New York, NY 10022

Maxwell Macmillan Canada, Inc.
1200 Eglinton Avenue East
Suite 200
Don Mills, Ontario M3C 3N1

Macmillan Publishing Company is part of the Maxwell Communication Group of Companies

First Edition

Printed in the United States of America

10 9 8 7 6 5 4 3 2 1

Created and Developed by The Learning Source

Acknowledgments
We would like to express our gratitude to the Imperial War Museum, London, England, for their assistance in locating and providing many of the photographs used in this book.

Photo Credits
Bettmann Archive: pp. 12, 15, 37, 40, 41, 43; Imperial War Museum: cover, pp. 4, 6, 8, 9, 17, 18, 21, 23, 24, 27, 30, 34; Smithsonian Institution: pp. 11 (Smithsonian Photo 87-9519), 19 (Smithsonian Photo 82-46-7), 38 (Smithsonian Photo 77-7353).

CONTENTS

CHAPTER 1

BENEATH THE STREETS
LONDON, ENGLAND, JUNE 1944

Air raid sirens blared loudly, and London, England, was on the alert. Searchlights swept the night sky, looking for enemy bombers that might come roaring over the city at any moment.

Except for the bright glare of the searchlights, the city was as dark as people could possibly make it. Street lamps were off. Cars drove without headlights. And dark, heavy curtains kept light from seeping through the windows of homes and places of business. Even the slightest flicker of light could offer an enemy bomber an inviting target.

Meanwhile, beneath the streets, a 12-year-old boy huddled beside his sleeping mother and sister. Along with hundreds of other people, he was crowded into a cold, concrete subway station. Like Londoners in other parts of the city, the boy and his family were trying to find shelter from a war that had been going on for nearly five years.

After each air raid, people of London came out of their shelters to see what was left of their city.

It had not always been like this, of course. Until several years before, people had lived normal lives. Families enjoyed the bright lights of their living rooms, and children played in the streets.

Then, in September 1939, the country went to war with Germany. Fathers, husbands, brothers, and sisters joined the army and the navy. The streets became quieter. But still, people did not live much differently than before.

A year later, on September 7, 1940, Germany's leader, Adolf Hitler, sent his air force winging over London. The terrible German bombings of London had begun.

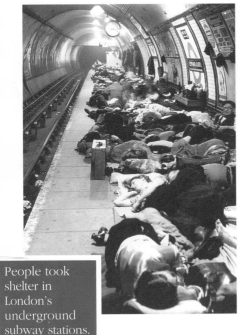

People took shelter in London's underground subway stations.

When the air raid sirens sounded, people raced to shelters in cellars and subway stations. There they were fairly safe. But they could still hear the German bombs falling on the city above them. They could also hear the thuds of British **antiaircraft guns** and the screams of British **fighter planes**. But, most of all, they heard quiet prayers and the voices of people reminding one another to be brave.

Day after day, night after night, the bombers came. With each new raid, more buildings were destroyed. Fires raged through buildings and whole neighborhoods. Entire families were wiped out within a few terrifying seconds.

The bombings went on for eight months. At one point, German planes pounded London for 57 nights in a row. During those months, the **blitz**, as the people of London called it, claimed the lives of about 23,000 people. But the residents of the city kept up their spirits. The people of London, they told each other, would survive the bombings— and anything else that their enemies had to offer.

Finally, in May 1941, Hitler called off his bombers. The air over London became quiet once again.

Life in the city did not return to normal, however. Food— and just about everything else—was in short supply. Rain, heat, and, later, cold weather battered the Londoners left homeless by the bombs. As people grew more desperate, looting and robbery became more common. Worst of all, though, was the fear that the bombings would begin again.

And they did. On January 17, 1943, German bombers roared in under the British defenses. Flying just above the rooftops, the planes dumped their bombs on the city of London. Then the planes raced back across the English Channel to the safety of German-held France.

Again and again the planes came. One attack buried 150 children during a lunch break at school. Another killed

As a rocket struck, Londoners ran for shelter.

300 people enjoying themselves at a dance hall.

Eventually, the second round of bombings came to an end, just as the first had. Now, almost a year after the last bombs fell, London's newspapers were promising that the city's troubles were nearly at an end. On June 6, 1944, British, American, and other **Allied** forces had landed in France. The war would soon be over... or so most of London and everyone else fighting against the Germans, Italians, and Japanese hoped.

Meanwhile, however, Hitler was boasting of a secret weapon. It was, the German leader said, more deadly than anything the world had ever seen. He claimed it would finish off his enemies once and for all.

All of London wondered what Hitler's mysterious wonder weapon could be. People heard rumors about strange, pilotless planes that had crashed to earth just a few miles from London. Were these Hitler's new wonder weapons? What damage could these weapons bring that was worse than what London had already suffered?

On the night of June 16, 1944, London found out. Amidst the darkness, a huge explosion shook the ground. But the blast didn't come from a bomb or even from a plane. It came from a new, terrifying weapon— a **rocket**— that the world would call the V-1.

Air raid wardens comforted London's children.

Soon the V-1 was joined by a more advanced rocket, the V-2, a pointed metal cylinder that shot through the sky at unbelievable speeds. The *V* in these two names stood for *vengeance*, or revenge. Adolf Hitler hoped that these new weapons would bring revenge for the recent defeats of German soldiers. But for the frightened 12-year-old boy hiding in a subway station, these terrible V-weapons were something else. They were the latest chapter in the long nightmare that had been taking place for almost one-third of his life.

THE SEEDS ARE SOWN
GERMANY, 1905–1932

M any years earlier, in 1905, another young boy spent restless nights, too. But his thoughts were not of bombs and death. Instead he dreamed of new worlds to discover and of travel to the stars.

Born in the Eastern European country of Romania, the boy was named Hermann Oberth. What inspired his dreams were two books by the French author Jules Verne, *From the Earth to the Moon* and *Travel to the Moon.* The books told of a trip to the moon on an amazing rocket-powered spaceship.

For years, Oberth thought about how to send a rocket into space. As he grew older, he began to study the subject seriously. By 1922, he had earned a master's degree at Heidelberg University in Germany.

Oberth also wrote a scientific report. Published in 1923, it was called "The Rocket into Interplanetary Space," and it was about travel between the planets. In it, Oberth described how to power rockets so that they could escape the pull of the earth's gravity and fly into outer space. This power, Oberth claimed, would come from burning liquid fuel and was called liquid propulsion.

Many of the scientists Oberth knew did not accept his ideas. But that didn't stop Oberth from continuing his work in the field of space travel.

Early attempts at rocket-making had used solid fuels such as powder. Solid fuel worked well for fireworks and other simple rockets. But it had serious limitations for powering a rocket over a great distance.

Oberth discovered that liquid fuel burned more slowly than solid fuel. This meant that liquid fuel was easier to control. It also meant that, pound

It took many years to get the V-2 to its launching pad.

for pound, liquid fuel could give more power to a rocket. And power was exactly what a rocket would need to break free of earth's gravity and travel into outer space.

Experimenting with liquid propulsion took time. Oberth spent years working on the project. As time went on, more people became interested in rockets and space travel. Rocket designers from around the world began sharing

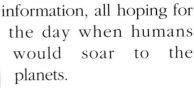

information, all hoping for the day when humans would soar to the planets.

Near Berlin, Germany's capital, a group called the Society for Space Travel was running its own rocket launching pad. It was called **Raketenflugplatz** (pronounced rah-KET-in-floog-plahtz), which means "rocket-flying place." During the 1930s it attracted the most knowledgeable people in the field of **rocketry**. Hermann Oberth quickly became one of the most important figures at the launchpad.

Wernher von Braun quickly became a leader in the German rocket program.

At the Berlin launchpad, Oberth met a brilliant high school student named **Wernher von Braun** (pronounced VERN-her fon BROWN). From an early age, von Braun had been fascinated by astronomy, the study of the stars, planets, and space. His mother had encouraged him by giving him a telescope. She also gave him books by Jules Verne and other science fiction writers. But it was Hermann Oberth's paper on space travel that really excited the young von Braun.

12

By 1932, von Braun was a student at Berlin University. He also was helping Oberth plan and test designs for a new rocket. But the Raketenflugplatz was nearly out of money.

Rocket materials and test flights were expensive. For a while, the scientists tried charging admission to their rocket launches, but these fees did not raise much cash. And when some rockets failed to get off the ground, some spectators even demanded their money back!

The scientists looked for help among German business leaders. Money from the business world was difficult to find, however. Times were hard in Germany, and hundreds of thousands of people were out of work. There was little money to spare for things like research. Besides, few people could see what rockets and outer space had to do with business.

Out of desperation, Germany's rocket scientists turned to the government for help. The government had special reasons to be interested in rocketry.

Germany had been badly beaten in World War I. In the treaty that was signed after that war, Germany was forced to pay a high price for its defeat. It had to give up some of its land and pay money to the countries it had invaded. Great Britain, France, Italy, the United States, and other countries that had defeated Germany also put strict limits on the number of warships, warplanes, and guns that Germany could have.

However, that peace treaty did not mention rockets. To the leaders of the German army, rockets were a way to get around the Allies' rules and make Germany's armed forces strong again.

The scientists at the Raketenflugplatz were beginning to achieve success with their rockets. In fact, two rockets, Mirak and Mirak II, were successful enough to make army leaders think that there just might be a future in rocketry. They chose a young officer named Walter Dornberger to find out.

Thirty miles south of Berlin, at the town of Kummensdorf, Dornberger set up a test site for rocket experiments. The army gave him $50,000 to start work on a rocket-powered weapon. It was not a lot of money. But it was enough to begin the work.

In 1932, Dornberger visited the Berlin launchpad. He, too, was impressed by young Wernher von Braun. In fact,

● Peenemünde

Berlin ●

Kummensdorf ●

GERMANY

The rocket program spread from Berlin to other places in Germany.

Dornberger offered the young man the job of managing the experiments at the new rocket station.

Von Braun considered Dornberger's offer very carefully. The rockets at the Berlin launchpad were toys compared with the ones Dornberger wanted. But von Braun dreamed of sending those new rockets to other planets—not to an enemy here on earth.

Walter Dornberger helped organize Germany's rocket program.

What *were* von Braun's dreams? Like Oberth, von Braun dreamed of a space station that would permanently orbit the earth. This space station would be people's first home in space. It would also be a base from which spaceships left for other planets.

Building weapons was a long way from this dream. But von Braun believed that the army's rockets could take him a step closer to his goal. So he decided to accept Dornberger's offer.

CHAPTER 3

THE WORK BEGINS
GERMANY, 1932–1937

A s soon as he could, von Braun went to work on the problems of liquid-fueled rockets. He began with this simple scientific law about how things move: *For every action there is an equal and opposite reaction.*

A common example of this is the flight of a party balloon. Imagine that you have filled a balloon with air. When you let go of the balloon, air begins to rush out of the open end. This is the "action." The air that is still inside the balloon pushes away from the escaping air. This is the "reaction" that sends the balloon flying.

Inside a rocket, the fuel is burned to produce a gas. The gas is forced out of the **exhaust** opening at an extremely high speed. This creates the power that lifts the rocket in the opposite direction into the sky.

As the rocket rises, the air becomes thinner. The thin air gives the rocket little **resistance**—and a longer, faster, easier flight is possible. There is so little resistance, in fact, that a rocket can coast at hundreds—or even thousands—of miles per hour. Then, once the rocket reaches its target, it can be guided back to earth.

The theory made sense. But actually building a rocket that could go high enough and far enough was a challenge.

By November 1, 1932, von Braun had set up shop at Dornberger's rocket station. Von Braun had little to go on. But he experimented endlessly. Eventually, he and the scientists who joined him learned from their successes—and from some unforgettable mistakes.

By the winter of 1932–1933, von Braun had an engine ready for testing. A special test stand with three long concrete walls was built for the engine. One wall had small holes through which people could watch.

In time, von Braun's rocketeers moved to a larger base.

Inside, surrounded by fireproof bricks, was the 20-inch engine itself. It stood **nozzle**-down, like a giant silver pear. It was expected to give 650 pounds of pushing power, called **thrust**.

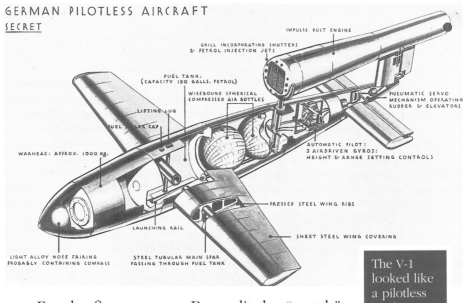

GERMAN PILOTLESS AIRCRAFT
SECRET

IMPULSE DUCT ENGINE

GRILL INCORPORATING SHUTTERS
& PETROL INJECTION JETS

FUEL TANK,
(CAPACITY 130 GALLS, PETROL)

WIREBOUND SPHERICAL
COMPRESSED AIR BOTTLES

PNEUMATIC SERVO
MECHANISM OPERATING
RUDDER & ELEVATORS

LIFTING LUG

FUEL FILLER CAP

AUTOMATIC PILOT:
3 AIRDRIVEN GYROS:
HEIGHT & RANGE SETTING CONTROLS

WARHEAD: APPROX. 1000 Kg.

PRESSED STEEL WING RIBS

LAUNCHING RAIL

SHEET STEEL WING COVERING

LIGHT ALLOY NOSE FAIRING
PROBABLY CONTAINING COMPASS

STEEL TUBULAR MAIN SPAR
PASSING THROUGH FUEL TANK

The V-1 looked like a pilotless airplane.

For the first test, von Braun lit the "match," a 12-foot rod with a can of gasoline at the end. The **valves** of the fuel tanks were opened, and von Braun put the match to the fuel.

In an instant, exhaust fumes built up inside the engine. The shiny, pear-shaped engine exploded in a blinding flash. The test stand was reduced to a heap of broken cement, splintered wood, and twisted steel.

The test was a failure. Von Braun and his assistants had to start over again. As they worked, the scientists faced problem after problem. At one point, they had too much oxygen inside the engine. This made the engine burn so hot that its aluminum tank melted.

The scientists also had to solve the problem of keeping the rocket on course. Dornberger wanted a rocket that could carry 2,000 pounds of explosives—and hit a target 160 miles away. Control was the key to this kind of accuracy. But how were the scientists to control the speeding rocket?

First, von Braun attached tail fins to the rocket, like feathers on the end of an arrow. The fins, he hoped, would keep crosswinds from blowing the rocket off course. But the fins would be of little or no use in the thin upper atmosphere, where there was practically no air for the fins to move through. So von Braun tried little wings that could control the air rushing out the exhaust nozzle. He also added a **gyroscope**, a spinning device that keeps its balance no matter how it is turned. The gyroscope would help keep the rocket steady. The plan seemed good. But would it work?

By December 1934, von Braun had two rockets, named Max and Moritz, ready for testing. One of these soared a mile and a half into the sky over the sea. Dornberger proclaimed the tests a success, and the German army gave von Braun more money for the project.

The rocket's controls rode in its nose cone.

The money was desperately needed for more research. Fins, wings, and gyroscopes were fine for controlling small rockets. But von Braun would need something else to control the giant rockets Dornberger wanted for the army.

Von Braun finally found his answer. He and his team designed an electric gyroscope. Inside the rocket, the gyroscope would be mounted on brackets. The brackets would let the gyroscope stay upright no matter how the angle of the rocket changed. By making the gyroscope tilt, von Braun could make the whole rocket tilt and change direction.

Finally, after months of work, von Braun was ready to see how his rocket and guidance system worked. But now the test site itself—just a few miles from the city of Berlin—became a problem.

Launching rockets near Germany's capital had grown risky. After all, an accident could put thousands of people in danger. And, just as important, the launchings would advertise what was supposed to be a top-secret operation.

Army money came through once again, this time to build a new research center. By April 1937, von Braun and his rocketeers moved to Peenemünde (pronounced Pee-nuh-MUHN-duh).

Located on an island in the Baltic Sea, Peenemünde seemed an unlikely place to build rockets. Wild birds

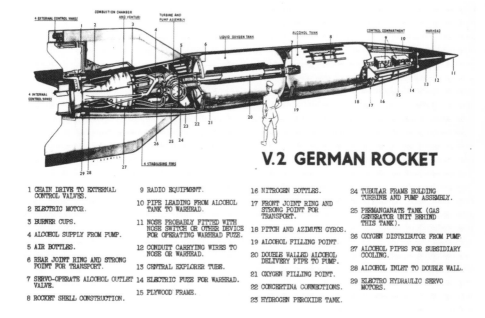

V.2 GERMAN ROCKET

1 CHAIN DRIVE TO EXTERNAL CONTROL VALVES.

2 ELECTRIC MOTOR.

3 BURNER CUPS.

4 ALCOHOL SUPPLY FROM PUMP.

5 AIR BOTTLES.

6 REAR JOINT RING AND STRONG POINT FOR TRANSPORT.

7 SERVO-OPERATE ALCOHOL OUTLET VALVE.

8 ROCKET SHELL CONSTRUCTION.

9 RADIO EQUIPMENT.

10 PIPE LEADING FROM ALCOHOL TANK TO WARHEAD.

11 NOSE PROBABLY FITTED WITH NOSE SWITCH OR OTHER DEVICE FOR OPERATING WARHEAD FUZE.

12 CONDUIT CARRYING WIRES TO NOSE OR WARHEAD.

13 CENTRAL EXPLORER TUBE.

14 ELECTRIC FUZE FOR WARHEAD.

15 PLYWOOD FRAME.

16 NITROGEN BOTTLES.

17 FRONT JOINT RING AND STRONG POINT FOR TRANSPORT.

18 PITCH AND AZIMUTH GYROS.

19 ALCOHOL FILLING POINT.

20 DOUBLE WALLED ALCOHOL DELIVERY PIPE TO PUMP.

21 OXYGEN FILLING POINT.

22 CONCERTINA CONNECTIONS.

23 HYDROGEN PEROXIDE TANK.

24 TUBULAR FRAME HOLDING TURBINE AND PUMP ASSEMBLY.

25 PERMANGANATE TANK (GAS GENERATOR UNIT BEHIND THIS TANK).

26 OXYGEN DISTRIBUTOR FROM PUMP.

27 ALCOHOL PIPES FOR SUBSIDIARY COOLING.

28 ALCOHOL INLET TO DOUBLE WALL.

29 ELECTRO HYDRAULIC SERVO MOTORS.

The V-2 was a complex machine.

nested in saltwater marshes. Deer grazed in nearby forests. But the setting was private. Thick woods would hide the launchpads. The trees would also hide the railway that would be built to carry supplies.

Most important, though, rockets at Peenemünde would roar out over the sea. This meant that few people would notice them. No one would be harmed, either. And when the rockets finally came down, the bottom of the sea made a good hiding place for the German army's secrets. ➤

CHAPTER

4

THE ARMY HOLDS THE PURSE STRINGS
GERMANY, 1934–1938

Secrets were important to the German army. But they had become even more important for Adolf Hitler.

In 1933, Hitler, the head of the **Nazi Party**, had become the leader of all Germany. By 1934 he had become the country's **führer**, its unquestioned dictator.

Hitler and the other Nazi leaders quickly began creating a "new" Germany. Concentration camps were built to hold Hitler's enemies—the people he blamed for all of Germany's problems. Jews, Gypsies, intellectuals, Communists, homosexuals, trade union members, and even members of other political parties were rounded up and carted away. The campaign of terror and murder known as the Holocaust was under way.

Surprisingly, von Braun and his rocketeers paid little attention to the German dictator and his crimes against humanity. They were busy dreaming of rockets, space

The huge V-2 had to be lifted into firing position.

stations, and travel between the planets. Von Braun didn't even think that Hitler was very dangerous. The dictator was, according to von Braun, just a loudmouthed fool with a funny-looking mustache.

Hitler did not think much of his rocket scientists, either. The German leader favored more surefire weapons — planes, submarines, and tanks. But because important officers in the German army *did* believe in the rocket project, money kept coming in for research and testing. Von Braun was soon making plans for a bigger, more powerful rocket.

Ready for launch, the V-2 was an awesome sight.

Using all their talents, brainpower, and skills, von Braun's scientists developed a new, jumbo-size rocket named A-4. The new rocket was 46 feet in length, about the size of a school bus. When filled with 9 tons of fuel and carrying its 1-ton warhead, it weighed about 13 tons.

The A-4 would not only be big. It would be fast, too. In just 65 seconds, the A-4 could rise to an altitude of 25 miles and travel faster than the speed of sound. Once in the thin upper atmosphere, the A-4 could streak along at 3,600 miles per hour.

To help it pass easily through the earth's atmosphere, scientist gave the A-4 a sleek, streamlined shape. Special care was also taken to get the A-4 back to earth. Hurtling down through the friction of the earth's atmosphere would be a broiling ride. So the A-4 was made as fireproof as possible.

Finally, the developers created a special fuel system. A rocket as fast as the A-4 needed a lot of fuel all at once. No equipment available at the time could do the job. So new pumps were designed and built. These pumps could send 3½ tons of alcohol and 5 tons of liquid oxygen into the engine during the rocket's first 65 seconds of flight.

As time went on, von Braun's team grew to over 100. Together, the scientists, engineers, and mechanics struggled along in their far-off island world. Valves, pumps, speed, and altitude filled every dinner conversation. Little mention was ever made of how deadly these rockets might be. Nor did anyone talk—or think—much about how many lives the rockets might claim if they were ever used in war.

By 1938 the A-4 was almost a reality. But its creators' minds were fixed firmly on the stars, not on the war that the A-4 was designed to fight. In 1938, however, that war was coming closer and closer. ➤

CHAPTER 5

THE ROUGH ROAD TO SUCCESS
1938–1943

Miles from Peenemünde, Adolf Hitler had another invention—one that he was much more eager to use than any rocket. Called **blitzkrieg** (pronounced BLITS-kreeg), it was a new, swift-moving kind of warfare. Hitler believed that the blitzkrieg would help him build a great German empire that would last a thousand years.

Over the years, Hitler had gained much territory for Germany. In 1936 he reclaimed German land that had been given to France after World War I. In March 1938 he forced Austria to become a part of Germany. Later that same year, he took over the country of Czechoslovakia.

Remarkably, Hitler achieved all this without a fight. Threats and trickery were his main weapons, and they worked surprisingly well.

By 1939, however, the German dictator was greedy for more—and bigger—conquests. And he was ready to use his new weapon, the blitzkrieg, to achieve his goals.

Rockets firing, a V-2 lifted slowly from the ground before streaking toward its target.

On September 1, 1939, Hitler unleashed his forces on Germany's next-door neighbor Poland. Tanks and armored troop carriers broke through Polish defenses. From overhead, German warplanes attacked Polish forces and leveled towns and cities.

Poland's allies—France, Great Britain, and others—were bound by treaty to help. France and Britain quickly declared war on Germany. But it was too late for Poland. Within days, the country was defeated, and the Nazis took control.

Soon Hitler's forces were on the attack elsewhere. In six months the blitzkrieg overran six European countries, including Norway, Denmark, Belgium, and the Netherlands. By June 14, 1940, German troops marched into Paris, the capital of France. Great Britain lay just a few miles away, across the English Channel. Hitler and his armies were eager for the battle.

Meanwhile, the scientists at Peenemünde made slow progress. A 1-ton rocket was sent to an altitude of 2½ miles. It then parachuted to sea 8 miles away from its launchpad.

The rocket hadn't reached the speed of sound or traveled any great distance. But its guidance system had worked perfectly. Von Braun was encouraged.

Not all the Peenemünde scientists were encouraged, though. As time went on, some of the scientists grew uneasy about Hitler and the weapon they were making for him. At least one of them was worried enough to take action.

Late in 1939, a package was found outside the British embassy building in Oslo, Norway. Half-buried in the snow, it became known as the Oslo Report. The report was signed simply, "from a well-wishing German scientist." It described new German weapons—radar systems, glider

All Europe soon felt the effects of Hitler's war.

bombs, and a long-range rocket bomb called the A-4. The report even named Peenemünde as the site at which the A-4 was being created.

British officials read the Oslo Report carefully. But they did not take the news seriously. The story was too fantastic to be believed. So the German scientists at Peenemünde were left alone.

While von Braun's scientists worked, Hitler set out to conquer Britain—with a blitz, not rockets. By late summer of 1940, the blitz—full-scale bombing—was raging. Bomb after bomb fell on London and other British communities.

Meanwhile, planes from the British and German air forces were waging a fierce battle in the skies over England. Although it was outnumbered, Britain's Royal Air Force had better planes and pilots than the Germans. During the early days of the fighting, they shot down so many German planes that the German air force had to give up daytime bombing completely.

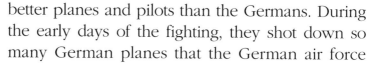

Rockets were built in underground factories.

By the middle of 1941, Hitler and his generals realized that bombs alone were not going to win the war, and they called them off.

More than 2,500 German planes had been knocked down, along with most of Germany's best pilots. The losses left Germany open to attack from Allied planes. Soon Germany itself was feeling the pain and terror of nightly bombings.

The Allies' main targets were Berlin and other key German cities. Peenemünde was spared. But von Braun's scientists felt the effects of the bombings, too. The supply of oil dwindled. Alcohol—needed for the A-4's rocket fuel—was almost impossible to get. So was liquid oxygen, another important part of the A-4's fuel.

Watching these events, Walter Dornberger was more convinced than ever that the A-4 could save Germany. Bombers cost Germany over $1 million each, and they averaged only six missions before they were shot down. An A-4 rocket cost a mere $38,000. Just as important, because an A-4 had no pilot or crew, no lives would be risked.

To von Braun and Dornberger, the future of all rocketry now depended on showing just what the A-4 could do. In June 1942 they got their chance. One of Hitler's key advisers, Albert Speer, was invited to a test launch.

As Speer watched, a giant A-4 rose from its launchpad and pushed upward into the sky. Just seconds into its flight, however, disaster struck. For some reason, the A-4 started tumbling like a baton, spinning back to earth.

What went wrong? The rocketeers checked carefully. It did not take them long to find the answer. It was just a minor problem in the guidance system. The A-4 was basically okay. Still, minor problems remained, and the A-4 failed its next round of tests as well.

On October 3, 1942, the team was ready for what everyone knew would be the final verdict on the A-4. If the rocket did not fly well and hit its target, there was little chance that Hitler would continue to pour money into the project.

As launch time neared, scientists, engineers, and firefighters waited anxiously. Speer was absent. But Hermann Oberth was there. So were movie cameras, which were busily recording the event.

One by one the seconds of the countdown ticked away. Finally the firing switch was pulled. For two seconds the 13.5-ton rocket did not move. Then, with a roar, the prayers of Dornberger, von Braun, and hundreds of others were answered.

Within five seconds, the A-4's engine had generated over 650,000 horsepower and was pounding out 25 tons of thrust. Flaming gases—burning at 5,100 degrees Fahrenheit—shot from the rocket's nozzle. As cameras and binoculars followed its path, the rocket slowly lifted from the launchpad.

At a height of 70 feet, the rocket hung in the air at an angle. Would it tumble and crash like others had done? Not this time. The crowd watched anxiously as the rocket kept climbing and climbing. It soared to a height of over 50 miles and raced toward its target at 3,300 miles per hour.

As the A-4 headed back to earth, a plane went to check the flight. A few moments later came the report. The A-4 had performed perfectly—all the way to its target. Tears of joy filled scientists' eyes. "Today the spaceship is born!" one cried.

But war, not spaceships, was in the minds of Germany's leaders. ➤

CHAPTER

6

THE TERROR IS LET LOOSE
1943–1945

During the summer of 1943, Dornberger and von Braun met with Hitler at the dictator's headquarters. They showed the film of the A-4's successful flight. Dornberger described how destructive the rocket could be. The German leader was so impressed that he completely changed his mind about rockets.

Hitler now wanted hundreds of rockets flying against Britain—immediately. But von Braun believed that he needed three more years to get his rocket ready. The rocketeers would have to pull off a miracle to get the job done.

Government money poured into Peenemünde. A large factory was built south of the island. Other factories were set up in Germany and Austria. Dornberger even began training soldiers to launch the missiles.

In the meantime, however, pilots from Britain's Royal Air Force had flown over Peenemünde and sighted long, finned objects. On August 17, 1943, Allied bombers attacked

Peenemünde. More than seven hundred people were killed. Among the dead were two important scientists and hundreds of Russian prisoners of war who had been forced to labor at Peenemünde. The test stands, wind tunnel, and guidance control laboratory, however, survived the attack.

For protection, Hitler moved the German rocket program to a secret underground spot in the Harz Mountains. There, 800 feet beneath the surface of the earth, inmates from a concentration camp labored to put together A-4s.

Time, though, was running out for both Hitler and von Braun. Allied bombs were raining down on cities all over Germany. Even Berlin, the German capital, was running low on electricity, food, and water.

Then, on June 6, 1944, the Allies landed their forces on the beaches of Normandy, in northwestern France. Fighting a lightning war of their own, the Allies pushed across France. Allied victory seemed near.

Still, Hitler raged on about vengeance and victory. Even with Berlin in ruins and his armies on the retreat, the dictator declared that a German triumph was at hand. He announced that at any moment the vengeance weapon would be ready. Then he would destroy his enemies once and for all.

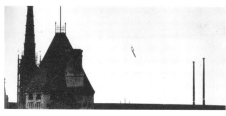

Sputtering loudly, V-1s dove at their targets.

The rocketeers, however, were not ready. Change after change was made in the A-4. The rocket was put through test after test. Though many of the flights went as planned, more than half of them failed. Again and again, A-4s either exploded or missed their targets. Von Braun rushed to help with the tests personally. Joking, Dornberger warned the young scientist to be sure to stand at the safest point: in the bull's-eye of the target.

In early June 1944, one rocket strayed so far off course that it landed on Swedish soil. Pieces of the rocket were collected and shipped to Britain, where they were examined by both British and American rocket specialists. The Allies now knew what Hitler's "wonder weapon" was—and they braced themselves for what was to come.

When the attacks came, however, they were not made by the A-4. They were made by the V-1, a small, pilotless jet plane carrying a ton of explosives.

As a weapon, the V-1 had two major problems. First, it was not very accurate. In fact, of the first 10 V-1s fired at Britain, only 4 made their way to British soil.

Second, the V-1 made a strange, sputtering sound that quickly earned it dozens of nicknames, including *doodlebug* and *buzz bomb*. Problems with sound and accuracy, however, did not change the fact that the V-1s were awesome weapons. Between June 13, 1944, and March 29, 1945, more than 8,000 V-1 missiles were launched against London. About 2,400 hit the area. Some were shot down by fighter planes and antiaircraft guns. Others crashed by themselves. But enough found their way to their targets to kill 6,139 people, injure 40,000 more, and destroy 75,000 buildings.

As the summer of 1944 ended, a second wave of destruction struck. On September 8, 1944, Hitler unleashed his real "wonder weapon."

Renamed the V-2, the A-4 missiles were launched from the Netherlands, which was still controlled by the Nazis. Soon, rocket after rocket was speeding toward Britain, making the 200-mile journey in less than five minutes. For six months, the people of London lived with a terror that could not be seen or heard—until it was too late. The V-2 was so fast that antiaircraft gunners and pilots could not see it in time to shoot it down. And, unlike the V-1, the V-2 made no sound to warn people of its coming. Instead, it raced ahead of its own sound, and its frightening whine could not be heard until just seconds before the rocket came crashing to earth.

Hitler finally had his wonder weapon, something that could win a victory for the German armies. But he had waited too long to throw his full support behind the rocketeers. His forces did not have enough V-2s to defeat Britain—or anyone else. And the V-2 went into battle before it was fully ready. As a result, many of the rockets failed to operate properly.

The last of the V-2s fell on London in March 1945. It killed 380 people. But by then the war was almost over. Two months later, Allied troops marched into Berlin. Hitler commited suicide rather than surrender.

As the Allies took control of Germany, top Nazis were arrested. Many of the people who had made weapons for Hitler faced charges of war crimes.

Hitler's rocketeers faced a different fate, however. Although they quickly surrendered to the Allies, the scientists who gave Hitler his wonder weapon were not tried as war criminals. They—and what they knew— were too valuable.

Von Braun and his rocketeers surrendered to the Allies.

Within a few months, von Braun and a team of more than 100 German rocket scientists were safely in White Sands, New Mexico. They soon taught the U.S. military all they knew about rockets. Other members of von Braun's old team found themselves in the Soviet Union. There they, too, were soon working on new, more powerful rockets.

ROCKETING INTO THE FUTURE
1946–1977

Between 1946 and 1951, Wernher von Braun and the scientists at White Sands launched 70 V-2s. Each flight provided the United States with valuable information about missiles.

In those days, American scientists knew far less about rockets and missiles than did von Braun's rocketeers. But the Americans learned quickly. And they had the support of the U.S. government. Like the German government before it, however, the United States was more interested in weapons than in space travel. This time, it was fear of the Soviet Union that pushed rocketry forward.

In 1952 von Braun became technical director of the U.S. Army **ballistic weapon** program. With his help, the United States developed a range of guided missiles. The Redstone, Juno, Pershing, and Jupiter-C missiles were all intended for war. And they were far more powerful than anything von Braun and his rocketeers had dreamed of during the 1930s.

American and German scientists began experiments with captured V-2s.

Von Braun might have continued in this way except for a tiny Soviet space satellite named *Sputnik*. Although both the United States and the Soviet Union had begun programs to explore space, the Soviet Union had the first really important success. In 1957 *Sputnik* was launched into space and circled the earth.

Americans were shocked. Within months, the United States was in a space race with the Soviet Union. Wernher von Braun was called upon to help his new country catch up—and win—the race.

Von Braun shared his dream of space travel with millions of people.

Government money poured in. This time, however, the money was being used for what von Braun had always wanted—space research. During the 1950s, von Braun became well-known throughout the United States. He traveled, gave lectures, appeared on TV and radio, and wrote books—all to publicize the American space program.

One of von Braun's books, *The Mars Project*, described a mission to the planet Mars made by 10 spaceships and a

New, larger rockets carried von Braun's dreams into space.

crew of 70. The book filled young people with the same dreams of space travel that had inspired young Hermann Oberth and Wernher von Braun.

In 1958 the U.S. government formed the National Aeronautics and Space Administration (NASA) to carry out the American space program. Wernher von Braun left the army and became director of NASA's flight center in Huntsville, Alabama. There he oversaw the creation of new Saturn rockets.

These Saturn rockets had several "stages," or boosters, and they made the old V-2s look like firecrackers. In 1961 the Saturn rocket launched a space capsule containing the first American astronaut, Alan Shepard Jr. Another Saturn rocket was used in 1962 to lift astronaut John Glenn into orbit around the earth. For eight years, von Braun and NASA experimented and tested. During that time, they explored the areas of space closest to the earth.

Finally, after eight years, they were ready for the flight that had sparked the dreams of Oberth, von Braun, and thousands of others. In July 1969, a Saturn rocket launched another capsule into space. And on July 20, two Americans, Neil Armstrong and Edwin Aldrin Jr., became the first humans to set foot on the moon.

Von Braun had even more in store for the world. In 1972, he left NASA to work in private industry. But the work he started went on. In 1973 the Skylab space station went into orbit. Circling the earth miles up in space, Skylab performed an amazing series of experiments. For six years it gathered information on the earth's environment, took photographs of the sun, and taught scientists the ins and outs of living and working in space.

In 1973, Skylab went into orbit, fulfilling von Braun's and Oberth's dreams of a space station.

Wernher von Braun died in 1977, before some of the most famous advances in space exploration took place. But he had lived to see the dream of an earth-orbiting space station come true. During his lifetime, humans finally broke free of the earth and began to explore the millions of miles of space around them. It was, as von Braun told audiences everywhere, a grand adventure. But, as the German-born scientist knew well, it was an adventure that had started with one of history's most terrifying weapons—the V-2 rocket.

GLOSSARY

air raid siren ➘ An alarm that warns people when enemy planes are near.

Allied ➘ Refers to Great Britain, France, the Soviet Union, the United States, and other nations. In World War II, the Allied powers were fighting Germany, Italy, and Japan.

antiaircraft gun ➘ A gun designed to shoot down airplanes.

ballistic weapon ➘ A weapon, like a missile or a rocket, that is launched into the air.

blitz ➘ The German word for "lightning." It was used to describe the German bombing of London and other cities during World War II.

blitzkrieg ➘ A word meaning "lightning war." During World War II, the Germans used a combination of tanks, airplanes, and fast-moving troops to quickly overrun their enemies.

exhaust ➘ The used gas or vapor escaping from an engine.

fighter plane ➘ A plane designed for combat against land troops, bombers, and other planes.

führer ➘ A German word for "leader."

gyroscope ➘ A spinning device that tends to resist any change in the direction in which it is standing.

Nazi Party ➘ The political party led by Adolf Hitler. The word is short for *National Socialist Workers' Party* in German.

nozzle ➘ The tip on a pipe or hose, through which liquid, gas, or solids can come out.

Raketenflugplatz ➘ A rocket launching area near Berlin, Germany.

resistance ➘ A force working against another force.

rocket ➘ A flying object with fuel inside. When the fuel burns, the object moves forward as a reaction to the gases released out the back of the object.

rocketry ➘ The study of rockets.

thrust ➘ The power to push.

valve ➘ A moving part that controls the flow of a gas or liquid.

von Braun, Wernher ➘ German-born scientist who helped develop Germany's V-weapons. Later he was a leading figure in the early days of the U.S. space program.

FURTHER READING

Cooksley, Peter G. *Flying Bomb.* North Vancouver, British Columbia: Encore Editions, 1979.

Henshall, Phillip. *Hitler's Rocket Sites.* New York: St. Martin's Press, 1985.

Huzel, Dieter K. *Peenemunde to Canaveral.* Westport, Connecticut: Greenwood Press, 1981.

Kennedy, Gregory. *Vengeance Weapon 2: The V-2 Guided Missile.* Washington, D.C.: Smithsonian Institute Press, 1985.

Lampton, Christopher. *Wernher von Braun.* Chicago: Watts, 1988.

Posin, Daniel Q. *Exploring and Understanding Rockets and Satellites.* Chicago: Benefic Press, 1967.

INDEX

13
14
17
18
20